AUTOMATING YOUR FOREX TRADES

FROM A BEGINNER TO A PROFESSIONAL

STEP BY STEP GUIDE ON HOW TO START AND
MONITOR AUTOMATED TRADES, BENEFITS OF
AUTOMATED TRADING SYSTEMS AND PITFALLS OF
AUTOMATION IN FOREX

EXPLOIT KNOWLEDGE

TABLE OF CONTENT

PREFACE

Introduction to Forex Automation

Overview of Automated Trading

The world of Forex trading has undergone a significant transformation with the introduction of automation, marking a revolutionary departure from the traditional manual strategies that were once prevalent among traders. This book starts by delving into the core of automated Forex trading—its definition, execution, and the technological advancements that have made it more accessible and efficient. We explore the historical shift from traditional to automated trading, emphasizing the technological progress that has transformed the Forex industry. This story not only establishes the context but also demonstrates the significant influence automation has had on improving trading efficiency and increasing market participation.

Benefits of Automation

Automated trading systems offer a wide range of benefits, with one of the most notable being the exceptional efficiency they bring to the trading process. This section highlights the major advantages of utilizing these systems, including the ability to operate non-stop, taking advantage of opportunities that go beyond time zones and regular market hours. In addition, the use of automation helps to eliminate emotional bias from trading decisions, promoting a more disciplined and consistent approach to Forex trading.

How This Book Will Help You

Educational Goals:

We are dedicated to providing you with a thorough understanding of automated Forex trading. This book is designed to help you improve your knowledge and expertise in trading; starting from the basics of setting up automated trading systems to exploring advanced trading strategies.

Practical Applications:

In addition to theoretical knowledge, this book places a strong emphasis on practical application. You will receive comprehensive guidance on choosing the appropriate trading software, setting up your system, and creating successful trading strategies. Every chapter is carefully crafted to build upon the previous one, creating a seamless and hands-on learning journey.

Resource for Success:

With practical examples, in-depth analysis, and expert advice, this book is a valuable resource for anyone looking to excel in the Forex market. Whether you're refining your existing systems or beginning anew, the resources and expertise offered here are designed to assist you in your trading pursuits.

Who Should Read This Book?

Aspiring Forex Traders:

If you're just starting out in the world of Forex trading, this book will provide you with a strong understanding of the market fundamentals and the intricacies of automation. It's designed to provide you with the essential tools to begin with confidence.

Seasoned Traders:

If you have experience in manual Forex trading, this guide provides valuable insights on how to improve your existing automated trading systems or make the transition to automated trading. Explore innovative strategies and cutting-edge technologies to rejuvenate your trading approach.

Financial Experts:

Professionals in the financial sector will find this book to be a valuable resource, providing insights and guidance from experts in the field. It offers a comprehensive exploration of the cutting-edge technologies and strategies that are influencing the direction of automated Forex trading.

Tech Enthusiasts:

If you have a strong passion for technology, especially in the realm of software, algorithms, and artificial intelligence in financial markets, this book demonstrates how these tools can be utilized to attain significant advantages in Forex trading.

As we begin our exploration of the complex realm of automated trading in the Forex market, this introduction lays the foundation for what lies ahead. This text guarantees all readers, regardless of their previous experience with Forex trading, that they are on the right track to becoming skilled in utilizing automation to achieve success in trading.

CHAPTER 1

UNDERSTANDING FOREX TRADING

Introduction

Let's delve into the fundamental elements, starting with the fundamentals of how the Forex market functions, moving on to the major currencies and trading pairs, and concluding with the specific jargon employed by traders across the globe.

Basics of Forex Markets

Forex trading presents an opportunity to participate in a global marketplace that is not only the largest financial market by trading volume but also one of the most fluids. What you need to know:

Market Structure

Decentralized Nature: Forex lacks a centralized exchange, functioning instead through a worldwide network of computers and brokers.

Market Participants: Includes large banks, hedge funds, commercial companies, central banks, and retail traders.

Trading Volume: Exceeds $6 trillion per day, making it the largest financial market globally.

Trading Hours and Sessions

24-Hour Market: Runs 24 hours a day during weekdays, closing only on weekends.

Global Sessions: Includes the Sydney session, Tokyo session, London session, and New York session, each with unique characteristics and trading volumes.

Factors Influencing Forex Markets

Economic Indicators: GDP reports, employment figures, and interest rate decisions.

Political Events: Elections, policy changes, and international negotiations.

Market Sentiment: Traders' perceptions and reactions to global events.

Major Currencies and Trading Pairs

Understanding the major currencies and how they pair for trading is fundamental to both manual and automated Forex trading strategies:

Major Currencies:

The US Dollar (USD): Involved in about 80% of all Forex transactions.

The Euro (EUR), Japanese Yen (JPY), British Pound (GBP), and others: Each plays a critical role in the financial markets.

Currency Pairs:

Major Pairs: Such as EUR/USD, USD/JPY, and GBP/USD, generally have lower spreads and are highly liquid.

Minor and Exotic Pairs: Include currencies from smaller economies paired with a major currency, typically more volatile and less liquid.

Characteristics of Trading Pairs:

Volatility: Different pairs exhibit varying levels of volatility based on economic, political, and market factors.

Liquidity: Major pairs are more liquid, making them generally more suitable for beginners and automated trading systems.

Understanding Forex Terminology

Mastering the language of Forex is key to effective trading. Familiarity with these terms will enhance your ability to deploy and manage automated trading systems:

Basic Terms:

Pip: The smallest price move that a given exchange rate can make based on market convention.

Lot Size: Standard trading units in the Forex market. A standard lot is 100,000 units of the base currency.

Operational Terms:

Leverage: Allows traders to gain a larger exposure to the market than the amount they deposited to open a trade.

Margin Call: A demand from a broker for additional funds or other collateral, in case the equity in the account falls below required levels due to trading losses.

Trading Costs:

Spread: The cost built into the buying and selling price of the currency pair.

Commissions: Fees charged by brokers for trading services.

Having a solid grasp on these fundamental aspects of Forex trading is crucial, especially if you are contemplating automating your trades. This understanding forms the basis for creating advanced trading strategies that can effectively navigate the ever-changing landscape of the global Forex market. As we continue reading this book, we will explore further how you can utilize this information to establish and oversee automated trading systems with efficiency and effectiveness.

CHAPTER 2

THE RISE OF AUTOMATED TRADING

Introduction

Automated trading has revolutionized the way Forex markets operate, introducing efficiencies and strategic capabilities that were unimaginable a few decades ago. In this chapter, we explore the history and evolution of automated trading, examine current trends, and discuss the potential future of automation in the Forex market.

History and Evolution of Automated Trading

Automated trading systems, also known as algorithmic trading, use computer algorithms to execute trades based on predefined criteria. How it has evolved:

Early Development:

1980s-1990s: The inception of automated trading can be traced back to when computers were first used to create trading systems. Early systems were rudimentary and often exclusive to institutional traders.

Advancements in Technology: As technology progressed, so did the complexity and capabilities of automated systems, enabling them to analyze vast amounts of data and execute trades at speeds impossible for humans.

Mainstream Adoption:

2000s: The adoption of electronic trading platforms made automated trading accessible to a broader audience, including retail traders.

Regulatory Changes: Shifts in regulations opened up the markets to high-frequency trading (HFT), a form of automated trading characterized by high speeds, high turnover rates, and high order-to-trade ratios.

Current Trends in Forex Automation

Automation in Forex trading is not just a passing trend but a significant evolution that continues to grow:

Algorithmic Trading:

Strategies: Includes statistical arbitrage, market making, and trend following, among others.

Tools and Technologies: Use of AI and machine learning to predict market movements more accurately and manage risks better.

High-Frequency Trading (HFT):

Impact on the Market: HFT strategies can dominate short-term trades in liquid markets, often sparking debates about their effect on market volatility and integrity.

Technological Race: Continual advancements in technology drive HFT firms to compete on the basis of speed and information processing capabilities.

Retail Traders and Automation:

Accessibility: Tools like MetaTrader have democratized access to sophisticated automated trading systems.

Community Development: Growing communities of developers and traders share strategies and tools, further enhancing capabilities and adoption.

Future Outlook

The future of automated trading in Forex looks robust, driven by technological advancements and increasing trader sophistication:

Integration of Advanced Technologies:

Artificial Intelligence and Machine Learning: These technologies are set to become more prevalent, providing systems the ability to learn from market data and adapt strategies in real time.

Blockchain and Decentralized Finance (DeFi):

Potential integration could increase transparency and reduce transaction costs.

Regulatory and Ethical Considerations:

Increased Scrutiny: As automated systems become more dominant, regulatory bodies may impose stricter guidelines to ensure market fairness and transparency.

Ethical Trading Practices: The need for ethical considerations in algorithm development will become more pronounced to prevent manipulative practices.

Expansion in Global Markets:

Emerging Markets: As markets in developing countries become more integrated into the global financial system, automated trading will play a significant role in their evolution.

Cross-Market Strategies: Automation may expand to encompass multi-asset strategies, including simultaneous trading in Forex, stocks, and commodities.

The path of automated trading is undeniably leading towards greater intricacy and incorporation of state-of-the-art technologies. Gaining a deep understanding of this ever-changing landscape is crucial for Forex traders who want to use automation to gain a strategic edge and stay ahead in a rapidly evolving market. As we explore further into the process of setting up and maximizing automated trading systems in the upcoming chapters, it is important to consider the historical insights, current trends, and future possibilities. By doing so, we can fully leverage the potential of automation in Forex trading.

CHAPTER 3

BENEFITS OF AUTOMATED FOREX TRADING

Introduction

Automated Forex trading systems offer distinct advantages that are not typically achievable through manual trading. From enhancing consistency to leveraging high-speed operations and refining strategies through backtesting, automation transforms the trading experience. This chapter explores these key benefits and explains why many traders are moving towards automation.

Consistency in Trading

One of the most significant advantages of automated trading is its ability to maintain consistency. How it helps:

Removal of Emotional Decision-Making:

Objective Trading: Unlike humans, automated systems do not suffer from fear or greed. They execute trades based solely on data and pre-defined criteria, ensuring decisions are not influenced by emotions.

Discipline in Volatile Markets: Automated systems adhere to the trading plan without hesitation, which is particularly valuable in highly volatile market conditions where human traders might second-guess their decisions.

Implementation of Complex Strategies:

Multi-Variable Trades: Automated systems can handle complex strategies that involve multiple variables and conditions faster and more efficiently than a human trader.

Consistent Application: Once a strategy is set, it can be consistently applied, trade after trade, ensuring systematic execution without fatigue or deviation.

Speed and Efficiency

The ability of automated trading systems to execute orders at high speeds is unmatched by human traders:

Rapid Order Execution:

Instant Market Response: Automated systems can process market data and execute trades within milliseconds. This speed is crucial in a market where price changes happen rapidly and can make a significant difference in trade outcomes.

Simultaneous Orders: Automation allows the execution of multiple orders at the same time across various markets, which maximizes opportunities and increases efficiency.

Optimization of Entry and Exit Points:

Precision Timing: Automated systems can monitor and react to market conditions continuously, allowing for precision in entering or exiting trades at the most opportune moments.

Slippage Reduction: Faster execution reduces the risk of slippage (the difference between the expected price of a trade and the price at which the trade is actually executed), thus potentially improving trade results.

Backtesting and Strategy Refinement

Automated trading not only executes trades but also offers powerful tools for strategy development and refinement:

Rigorous Backtesting Capabilities:

Historical Data Analysis: Automated systems can test trading strategies against historical market data to determine their viability before risking real capital.

Strategy Optimization: By adjusting parameters and testing different scenarios, traders can refine their strategies based on objective data, improving their effectiveness and adaptability.

Continuous Improvement:

Feedback Loops: Automated systems can be programmed to adapt and learn from past trades, incorporating lessons learned into future trading.

Algorithm Updates: As market conditions change, algorithms can be updated and optimized continuously to maintain their edge in the market.

The advantages of incorporating technology into trading practices are evident in automated Forex trading. It provides consistency, speed, efficiency, and the opportunity to thoroughly test and improve strategies. These systems not only improve operational capabilities, but also offer a platform for sustainable trading advantages in the highly competitive Forex market. As we progress, we will delve into the strategies for implementing and optimizing the advantages of automated trading systems.

CHAPTER 4:

CHOOSING YOUR AUTOMATED TRADING SOFTWARE

Introduction

Selecting the right automated trading software is a pivotal decision for any Forex trader. The choice between various platforms can significantly impact the effectiveness of your trading strategy and the overall trading experience. This chapter will guide you through the criteria for selecting trading platforms, provide an overview of popular systems, and discuss the pros and cons of custom versus off-the-shelf solutions.

Criteria for Selecting Trading Platforms

When choosing an automated trading platform, several key factors need to be considered to ensure it meets your trading needs:

Reliability and Performance:

Uptime: Ensures the platform operates continuously without crashes or downtime, which is crucial for round-the-clock Forex trading.

Execution Speed: Critical for minimizing slippage in fast-moving markets.

Usability and Support:

User Interface: Should be intuitive and easy to navigate, even for complex strategies.

Customer Support: Robust support is essential for resolving technical issues and answering trading queries.

Compatibility with Trading Strategies:

Customization Options: Ability to fine-tune and customize the trading algorithms according to your strategies.

Technical Indicators and Tools: Availability of advanced analytical tools and indicators for developing sophisticated trading strategies.

Cost and Fees:

Subscription Fees: Some platforms charge monthly or annual fees, while others might take a cut from your profits.

Transaction Fees: Consider the impact of transaction fees on your trading margins.

Overview of Popular Automated Trading Systems

Several automated trading platforms have gained popularity among Forex traders due to their reliability, feature sets, and user community:

MetaTrader 4 and 5 (MT4/MT5):

Widely Used: Among the most popular platforms in the Forex community.

Features: Offers robust charting tools, technical indicators, and a proprietary scripting language (MQL4/MQL5) for developing custom indicators and automated trading scripts.

NinjaTrader:

Versatility: Known for its advanced charting and trade simulation capabilities.

Community: Supports a large user community and extensive third-party development.

cTrader:

Algorithmic Trading Focus: Provides advanced order capabilities and high-quality analytics tailored for algorithmic trading.

Connectivity: Direct integration with interbank market rates and liquidity.

Custom vs. Off-the-Shelf Solutions

Choosing between custom and off-the-shelf trading software involves weighing the benefits of customization against the ease and reliability of tested solutions:

Custom Solutions:

Tailored Fit: Designed to suit specific trading strategies perfectly.

Flexibility: More adaptable to changing markets or unique trading conditions.

Cost and Time: Typically require more time and resources to develop and maintain.

Off-the-Shelf Solutions:

Quick Setup: Ready to use immediately with minimal setup.

Proven Reliability: Tested by a wide user base, offering a level of reliability and support.

Cost-Effective: Generally less expensive and require lower upfront investment than custom solutions.

It is important to select automated trading software that is in line with your trading strategy, experience level, and operational requirements. Through a thorough analysis of the platforms and weighing the pros and cons of tailored and pre-made solutions, you can choose a system that improves your trading efficiency and aligns with your long-term trading objectives. In the upcoming chapters, we will explore the process of configuring your selected software and fine-tuning it to achieve optimal performance.

CHAPTER 5

SETTING UP YOUR AUTOMATED TRADING SYSTEM

Introduction

Setting up an automated trading system involves technical preparation, integration with brokerage accounts, and stringent security measures. Proper configuration is crucial to ensure that your trading system operates efficiently and securely. This chapter provides a comprehensive guide to setting up your automated trading system with an emphasis on reliability and risk management.

Technical Requirements and Setup

Before launching an automated trading system, it's important to ensure that all technical aspects are addressed:

Hardware Requirements:

Processing Power: Adequate CPU and RAM to handle multiple tasks simultaneously without lag, which is crucial for high-frequency trading.

Reliable Internet Connection: A stable and fast internet connection to ensure continuous access to market data and seamless trade execution.

Software Installation:

Platform Compatibility: Check for compatibility with your operating system and ensure that all necessary software dependencies are installed.

Updates and Patches: Regularly update the software to incorporate new features and security patches.

System Configuration:

Parameter Settings: Configure trade parameters such as entry, exit, stop loss, and take profit instructions based on your trading strategy.

Algorithm Tuning: Fine-tune the algorithms to align with market conditions and trading goals.

Integrating Software with Brokerage Accounts

Proper integration of your automated trading software with your brokerage account is essential for real-time trading:

Account Setup:

Broker Selection: Choose a broker that offers robust API support for seamless integration with your trading platform.

API Configuration: Set up and test the API connection to ensure that your trading system can communicate effectively with your broker's platform.

Data Feeds and Execution:

Market Data Access: Ensure access to real-time market data feeds as latency can significantly impact trading performance.

Trade Execution Tests: Conduct tests to verify that trades are executed promptly and accurately according to your system's specifications.

Security Measures and Risk Management

Security and risk management are paramount in automated trading to protect your investments and personal information:

Security Protocols:

Encryption: Use strong encryption for data transmission to safeguard your trading data and account details.

Authentication Mechanisms: Implement multi-factor authentication for accessing the trading system.

Risk Management Tools:

Automatic Stop Losses: Set up automatic stop losses to limit potential losses on trades.

Risk/Reward Ratios: Establish risk/reward parameters that align with your trading strategy to manage exposure effectively.

Regular Monitoring and Updates:

System Checks: Regularly monitor the system's performance and adjust as needed to maintain optimal trading conditions.

Security Updates: Stay updated with the latest security practices and apply them to protect against new vulnerabilities.

Setting up your automated trading system is a detailed process that requires careful attention to technical settings, integration, security, and risk management. By meticulously configuring and maintaining your system, you can maximize its efficiency and safeguard your trading activities against potential risks. The next chapters will delve deeper into optimizing your system's performance and adapting to changing market conditions.

CHAPTER 6

DEVELOPING YOUR TRADING STRATEGY

Introduction

A well-crafted trading strategy is the backbone of successful automated trading. This chapter delves into the basics of Forex trading strategies, how to adapt these strategies for automated systems, and provides examples of profitable automated strategies. Understanding these elements will help you develop a robust strategy tailored to the dynamics of the Forex market.

Basics of Forex Trading Strategies

Before automating any strategy, it is essential to understand the fundamental approaches used in Forex trading:

Trend Following:

Principle: Capitalizes on the momentum of market trends.

Indicators: Commonly uses moving averages, MACD (Moving Average Convergence Divergence), and ADX (Average Directional Index) to identify trends.

Range Trading:

Principle: Focuses on currencies moving within a specific range.

Tools: Utilizes oscillators like RSI (Relative Strength Index) and stochastic indicators to find overbought or oversold conditions.

Scalping:

Principle: Makes numerous trades to profit from small price changes.

Approach: Requires very fast decision-making and execution, which makes it ideal for automation.

News Trading:

Principle: Exploits the volatility around news releases that impact the market.

Considerations: Requires systems capable of rapid response due to the quick market fluctuations following news announcements.

Adapting Strategies for Automation

Adapting manual trading strategies for automation involves several critical considerations:

Algorithm Design:

Precise Criteria: Define explicit rules for trade entries, exits, stops, and adjustments based on the strategy.

Error Handling: Incorporate mechanisms to manage and mitigate errors or unexpected market events.

Efficiency and Scalability:

Optimization: Fine-tune algorithms to ensure they are efficient and can handle high volumes of trades without lag.

Testing: Extensively backtest the strategy against historical data to validate its effectiveness over different market conditions.

Integration with Market Data:

Data Accuracy: Ensure the strategy uses accurate and timely market data to make informed decisions.

Latency: Minimize delays in data processing to maintain the strategy's relevance and effectiveness in fast-paced market environments.

Examples of Profitable Automated Strategies

Examples of strategies that have been successfully automated by traders around the world:

Dual Moving Average Crossover:

Strategy: Uses two moving averages (one short-term, one long-term). A trade is initiated when the short-term average crosses above (buy) or below (sell) the long-term average.

Automation: The system automatically executes trades when these crossovers occur, maximizing opportunities that come from these signals.

High-Frequency Trading (HFT) Strategies:

Strategy: Engages in rapid buying and selling of currencies using algorithms that capitalize on small price gaps.

Automation: Requires advanced computational technology to execute a large number of orders at extremely high speeds.

Arbitrage Opportunities:

Strategy: Exploits price discrepancies between different markets or derivatives.

Automation: Automatically detects and executes trades to profit from temporary price inefficiencies before they are corrected.

Developing a trading strategy for automation requires a deep understanding of Forex market mechanisms, strategic foresight, and technical expertise. By adapting your strategies for automation, you can take advantage of market opportunities with precision and speed. As you continue to refine your strategies and apply new technologies, your ability to succeed in the dynamic Forex market will enhance. The subsequent chapters will focus on monitoring and tweaking these strategies to stay aligned with changing market conditions.

CHAPTER 7

RISK MANAGEMENT IN AUTOMATED

TRADING

Introduction

Effective risk management is critical in automated Forex trading, as it helps protect against large unexpected losses and enhances the sustainability of your trading strategy. This chapter focuses on understanding leverage and margin, setting strategic stop-loss and take-profit points, and balancing risk with reward. These components are essential for maintaining control over the automated trading processes and ensuring long-term success.

Understanding Leverage and Margin

Leverage and margin are fundamental concepts in Forex trading that can significantly amplify both profits and losses:

Leverage:

Definition: Allows traders to control large amounts of currency with a relatively small amount of capital.

Implications: Increases the potential return on investment but also elevates the risk, making it possible to lose more than the initial investment.

Margin:

Definition: The deposit required to open and maintain a leveraged position, expressed as a percentage of the full position size.

Margin Call: Occurs when your account falls below the required margin level, prompting you to either add more funds or close positions to cover the margin deficit.

Managing Leverage and Margin:

Conservative Leverage: Use lower leverage ratios to reduce risk exposure.

Margin Monitoring: Continuously monitor margin levels and adjust positions as necessary to avoid margin calls.

Setting Stop-Loss and Take-Profit Points

Automated systems can be configured to use stop-loss and take-profit orders to manage risks effectively:

Stop-Loss Orders:

Purpose: Designed to limit an investor's loss on a position.

Implementation: Set at a percentage or price level that represents a tolerable loss, automatically closing the trade if the market moves unfavorably.

Take-Profit Orders:

Purpose: Used to lock in profits by closing a position once the market reaches a favorable price.

Implementation: Set at a price that achieves a desired profit level, ensuring gains are secured before market conditions can reverse.

Strategy Integration:

Automated Adjustments: Implement dynamic stop-loss and take-profit levels that can adjust based on changing market volatility or other indicators.

Backtesting: Regularly backtest to determine optimal stop-loss and take-profit settings under various market conditions.

Balancing Risk and Reward

Balancing risk and reward is essential to achieving long-term profitability in automated trading:

Risk/Reward Ratio:

Definition: A guideline that compares the expected returns of an investment to the amount of risk undertaken to capture these returns.

Application: Aim for a ratio that compensates adequately for the risk incurred. Common ratios include 1:2 or 1:3, where the potential reward is twice or three times the potential risk.

Diversification:

Across Instruments: Spread risk across different currency pairs to mitigate the impact of a loss in any single trade.

Strategy Diversification: Employ multiple trading strategies to smooth out performance over various market conditions.

Continuous Evaluation:

Performance Metrics: Use metrics like drawdown, expected payoff, win rate, and loss rate to evaluate and tune strategies.

Adjustment Triggers: Set parameters for automatic recalibration of strategies based on performance metrics or significant market events.

Risk management in automated trading is not merely about preventing losses but about optimizing the performance-to-risk ratio to ensure sustainable growth and profitability. By understanding and implementing strong risk management techniques such as managing leverage and margin, setting strategic stop-loss and take-profit points, and balancing risk with reward, traders can better navigate the complexities of the Forex market with automated systems. The following chapters will delve into monitoring system performance and making necessary adjustments to adapt to changing market dynamics.

CHAPTER 8

MONITORING AND ADJUSTING AUTOMATED

TRADES

Introduction

While automated trading systems can operate independently, active monitoring and timely adjustments are crucial to maintain effectiveness and adapt to changing market conditions. This chapter covers techniques for real-time monitoring of automated trades, guidelines on when to modify or exit a trade, and the importance of keeping a detailed trading journal.

Real-Time Monitoring Techniques

Effective real-time monitoring is essential for managing automated trading systems and ensuring they perform as expected:

Dashboard and Alerts:

Dashboard Setup: Utilize trading software with comprehensive dashboards that provide real-time insights into trade performance, system statistics, and market conditions.

Alert Systems: Set up customized alerts for significant events or indicators that could impact your trading strategy, such as abrupt price changes, unusual trading volumes, or margin calls.

Performance Metrics:

Tracking Efficiency: Regularly monitor key performance indicators like profit factor, maximum drawdown, and win-loss ratio.

System Health Checks: Monitor the operational status of your trading system, including connectivity, latency, and execution speed.

Market Conditions Analysis:

Market Sentiment: Keep an eye on overall market sentiment and significant economic announcements that could affect market volatility.

Correlation Watches: Track correlations between various currency pairs and adjust strategies to avoid risks associated with high correlation.

When to Modify or Exit a Trade

Knowing when to modify or exit a trade is as important as entering one. Automated systems need clear guidelines to make these decisions:

Modification Triggers:

Strategy Deviation: If the market behavior deviates significantly from the conditions for which the strategy was optimized, consider modifying the trade parameters.

Risk Management Adjustments: Modify stop-loss and take-profit points based on changing volatility or economic events.

Exit Criteria:

Stop-Loss Activation: Set up automated rules to exit a trade when a stop-loss level is hit to prevent further losses.

Profit Targets: Implement rules to exit a position when profit targets are reached to secure gains.

Manual Intervention:

Unforeseen Events: In cases of extreme market events or technical failures, manual intervention might be necessary to exit trades to protect the capital.

Keeping a Trading Journal

A detailed trading journal is a vital tool for refining strategies and tracking the progress of your automated trading:

What to Record:

Trade Details: Note down information about each trade, including entry and exit points, sizes, and outcomes.

Strategy Notes: Document the rationale behind each trading decision and strategy adjustments.

Analysis and Reflection:

Review and Learn: Regularly review the journal to understand what strategies are working and identify patterns in successful or unsuccessful trades.

Strategy Refinement: Use insights gained from the journal to refine and enhance your trading algorithms.

Continuous Improvement:

Feedback Loop: Incorporate lessons learned into future strategies, creating a continuous improvement loop that enhances overall trading performance.

Monitoring and adjusting automated trades are critical processes that ensure your trading system remains effective over time. By employing real-time monitoring techniques, understanding when to modify or exit trades, and meticulously keeping a trading journal, you can maintain control over your automated trading activities and continually enhance your strategies. The next chapters will explore advanced topics in automating Forex trading, providing deeper insights into maximizing the potential of automated systems.

CHAPTER 9

PITFALLS AND CHALLENGES OF AUTOMATED FOREX TRADING

Introduction

While automated Forex trading offers numerous advantages, it also comes with specific pitfalls and challenges that traders need to be aware of and manage effectively. This chapter explores common issues such as over-reliance on automation, technical failures, and the psychological aspects of trading with automation.

Over-Reliance on Automation

Automated trading systems can make trading easier, but over-reliance on these systems can lead to significant issues:

Complacency in Monitoring:

Risks: Traders may become complacent, assuming the system will manage all aspects of trading without fail.

Consequences: This can lead to missed signals for necessary intervention, resulting in unaddressed errors or misaligned trades.

Loss of Skill and Intuition:

Skill Atrophy: Relying too heavily on automation can lead to a decline in trading skills and intuition.

Balance: It's important to keep skills sharp by manually reviewing and understanding the trades and market conditions.

Technical Failures and Anomalies

Automated systems are not immune to technical failures, which can cause substantial disruptions:

Software Bugs and Glitches:

Impact: Errors in code or software malfunctions can lead to incorrect trades or loss of data.

Prevention: Regular software testing and updates are crucial to minimize this risk.

Connectivity Issues:

Internet Disruptions: Loss of internet connectivity can prevent new orders from being placed or existing ones from being closed.

Redundancy Plans: Have backup systems and alternative connectivity options like a mobile data connection to mitigate these risks.

Psychological Aspects of Automated Trading

The psychological impact of automated trading is often underestimated but can significantly affect trading outcomes:

Detachment from Trading:

Issue: Automation can lead to a lack of emotional engagement with trading, which might reduce vigilance.

Solution: Maintain regular check-ins and reviews to stay connected with the trading process.

Trust Issues:

Over-Trust: Traders may become overconfident in the infallibility of automated systems.

Under-Trust: Conversely, a lack of faith in the system's capabilities can lead to unnecessary manual interventions.

Balancing Trust: Develop a balanced view by understanding the system's mechanics and its limitations.

Stress from Losses:

Automated Losses: Watching a system incur losses can be stressful, especially if the trader doesn't fully understand the underlying strategies.

Coping Mechanisms: Building confidence in the system through backtesting and incremental live testing can help manage this stress.

Navigating the pitfalls and challenges of automated Forex trading requires a balanced approach that includes technical vigilance, continuous learning, and psychological readiness. By understanding these issues and preparing to address them proactively, traders can better harness the power of automation while minimizing its drawbacks. The final chapter will consolidate the knowledge gained and offer strategic advice on pursuing automated Forex trading successfully.

CHAPTER 10

ADVANCED CONCEPTS IN FOREX

AUTOMATION

Introduction

As traders become more proficient with automated Forex trading systems, delving into advanced concepts can provide a competitive edge and enhance trading performance. This chapter explores deeper into algorithm optimization, the integration of machine learning and artificial intelligence, and the effective use of economic indicators in trading strategies.

Algorithm Optimization

Optimizing trading algorithms is crucial for maintaining their effectiveness over time:

Parameter Tuning:

Purpose: Refining the parameters of a trading algorithm can help adapt to changing market dynamics.

Methods: Use grid searching, backtesting, and forward testing to identify the most effective settings for your trading strategy.

Adaptive Algorithms:

Flexibility: Develop algorithms that adjust their parameters automatically based on real-time market conditions.

Benefits: Increases the responsiveness of the trading system, potentially leading to higher profitability and reduced risk.

Machine Learning and AI in Forex

Machine learning and artificial intelligence are transforming how traders analyze data and make decisions:

Pattern Recognition:

Techniques: Utilize machine learning algorithms to identify complex patterns in historical data that are not readily apparent to human traders.

Application: Improve trade prediction accuracy by learning from past market behavior.

Predictive Analytics:

Forecasting: AI models can forecast market trends and price movements based on a vast array of inputs, including non-linear relationships that traditional models might overlook.

Real-Time Decision Making: AI can analyze large volumes of real-time data to make trading decisions faster than humanly possible.

Integration with Economic Indicators

Effectively integrating economic indicators into automated trading systems can significantly enhance strategy performance:

Automated News Trading:

Implementation: Develop algorithms that automatically parse and react to economic news releases, adjusting trades based on the expected impact on the market.

Challenges: Handling the volatility and false signals that can accompany news releases requires sophisticated algorithmic solutions.

Macro-Economic Indicators:

Key Indicators: Interest rates, employment reports, GDP growth, and inflation figures are among the macro-economic indicators that can influence currency strength and weaknesses.

Integration Strategy: Incorporate these indicators into your trading strategy to predict potential market movements and adjust trades accordingly.

Advanced concepts in Forex automation, such as algorithm optimization, the use of machine learning and AI, and the strategic integration of economic indicators, are essential for traders looking to enhance their competitive edge in the market. By embracing these sophisticated techniques, traders can build more robust, intelligent, and responsive trading systems capable of achieving superior results. As the field of Forex trading continues to evolve, staying ahead with these advanced concepts will be crucial for long-term success.

CHAPTER 11

REGULATORY AND ETHICAL

CONSIDERATIONS

Introduction

As automated Forex trading continues to grow in popularity and sophistication, understanding the regulatory frameworks and adhering to ethical trading practices become increasingly important. This chapter discusses these frameworks, highlights ethical considerations, and examines the impact of automation on the Forex market.

Understanding Regulatory Frameworks

Navigating the complex landscape of Forex regulations is crucial for compliance and successful trading:

Global Regulatory Bodies:

Examples: In the United States, the Commodity Futures Trading Commission (CFTC) and the National Futures Association (NFA) oversee Forex trading. Other countries have their own regulatory bodies, such as the Financial Conduct Authority (FCA) in the UK and the Australian Securities and Investments Commission (ASIC) in Australia.

Purpose: These organizations regulate the Forex market to prevent fraud, promote fair trading practices, and protect investor interests.

Compliance Requirements:

Licensing: Ensure that your broker is properly licensed and regulated by the appropriate authorities.

Reporting Obligations: Automated trading systems must adhere to reporting requirements, which may include disclosing trade execution data and strategy specifics.

Ethical Trading Practices

Maintaining high ethical standards is not only a legal obligation but also a cornerstone of sustainable trading strategies:

Transparency:

Honesty in Marketing: Clearly communicate the risks and potential outcomes of automated trading systems.

Disclosure of Algorithms: While the proprietary nature of algorithms can be protected, general operational frameworks should be transparent to ensure fair practices.

Preventing Manipulation:

Avoiding Price Manipulation: Algorithms must be designed to trade legitimately without creating false market movements or engaging in deceptive practices.

Monitoring for Abusive Strategies: Regular audits and checks should be implemented to ensure trading algorithms do not inadvertently or deliberately engage in market manipulation.

Impact of Automation on the Forex Market

The widespread adoption of automated trading technologies has profound implications for the Forex market:

Market Efficiency:

Increased Liquidity: Automated trading contributes to market depth and liquidity, making it easier for traders to enter and exit positions.

Price Discovery: Automation helps in the efficient discovery of prices by processing vast amounts of information quickly.

Volatility and Systemic Risk:

Potential for Flash Crashes: High-frequency trading and automated algorithms can sometimes lead to sudden market drops, known as flash crashes.

Systemic Risks: The interconnected nature of trading systems means that failures in one part can potentially affect the entire market.

Understanding and adhering to regulatory and ethical standards is essential for anyone involved in automated Forex trading. As automation technology evolves, so too will the frameworks and ethical considerations governing its use. It is imperative for traders to stay informed and engaged with these developments to ensure their trading practices remain compliant and ethical, ultimately contributing to a more stable and fair trading environment.

CHAPTER 12

BUILDING A LONG-TERM AUTOMATED

TRADING CAREER

Introduction

Sustaining a successful career in automated Forex trading requires more than just setting up systems and strategies. It demands continual learning, active networking, and an ability to stay ahead of market changes. This chapter provides insights into how you can build a lasting and prosperous career in this dynamic field.

Continual Learning and Adaptation

The Forex market is constantly evolving, making continual learning and adaptation crucial for long-term success:

Educational Resources:

Stay Updated: Regularly engage with new educational materials, such as books, courses, webinars, and conferences focused on Forex and automated trading.

Technology Trends: Keep abreast of the latest developments in trading technology and software to enhance your trading systems.

Adaptive Trading Strategies:

Testing New Algorithms: Regularly backtest and refine your trading algorithms to ensure they remain effective as market conditions change.

Flexibility: Be prepared to overhaul or adjust your strategies based on new economic data, market trends, or changes in market regulations.

Networking with Other Traders

Networking with peers in the trading community can provide support, insights, and opportunities for collaboration:

Online Trading Communities:

Forums and Social Media: Join forums, social media groups, and online platforms where traders discuss strategies, share insights, and update each other on market developments.

Webinars and Virtual Meetups: Participate in webinars and virtual meetups to connect with experienced traders and industry experts.

Professional Associations:

Memberships: Consider joining professional trading associations to gain access to exclusive resources, networking events, and educational seminars.

Conferences and Seminars: Attend industry conferences and seminars to meet other professionals, learn about the latest trends, and expose yourself to new ideas and strategies.

Staying Ahead in a Dynamic Market

To maintain a competitive edge, it's essential to proactively manage your trading approach and embrace innovations:

Market Research:

Regular Analysis: Conduct regular market analysis to understand potential impacts on the Forex market, including geopolitical events, economic announcements, and other market drivers.

Advanced Analytics: Utilize advanced analytical tools and techniques to forecast market movements more accurately.

Innovation and Technology:

Leveraging AI and Machine Learning: Incorporate more sophisticated AI and machine learning models to enhance predictive accuracy and decision-making processes.

Automation Enhancements: Continuously explore enhancements in automation technology to improve trading execution and efficiency.

Building a long-term career in automated Forex trading is an ongoing journey of education, adaptation, and active engagement with the trading community. By committing to continual learning, networking with other traders, and staying ahead of market trends and technological advancements, you can sustain and grow your trading career. This proactive approach will enable you to navigate the complexities of the Forex market and achieve long-term success.

Appendix

Glossary of Terms

A comprehensive glossary of Forex and automated trading terms to help familiarize new traders and serve as a reference for experienced practitioners:

Algorithmic Trading: The use of computer algorithms to execute trading orders with speed and efficiency based on pre-established trading strategies.

Backtesting: The process of testing a trading strategy on historical data to see how it would have performed in the past.

Drawdown: The reduction in account equity from a peak to a trough during a specific period for a trading account.

Forex (Foreign Exchange Market): The global decentralized market where currencies are traded. The Forex market is the largest, most liquid market in the world.

Leverage: The use of borrowed capital to increase the potential return of an investment.

Margin: The amount of capital required in an account to maintain a Forex trade.

Pip (Percentage in Point): A unit of measurement for the change in value between two currencies. For most pairs, a pip corresponds to a movement of 0.0001.

Scalping: A trading strategy that attempts to profit from small price changes, often executed rapidly and repeatedly.

Slippage: The difference between the expected price of a trade and the price at which the trade is actually executed.

Stop-Loss Order: An order placed with a broker to buy or sell once the stock reaches a certain price, designed to limit an investor's loss on a position.

Recommended Reading and Resources

A selection of books, websites, and other resources that provide valuable insights and further reading on automated Forex trading:

Books from the Author:

"Forex Trading Fundamentals: A Practical Guide to Understanding the Basics of Forex Markets, Currency Pairs And How Forex Trading Works For Beginners And Professionals" - Offers a deep dive into Forex Trading. https://a.co/d/8PPHqco

Websites:

Investopedia (www.investopedia.com) - Provides a wide range of educational articles, tutorials, and videos about Forex and trading strategies.

DailyFX (www.dailyfx.com) - Offers real-time forex news and market analysis.

Software Tools:

MetaTrader 4/5 - Popular platforms for automated trading, providing tools for technical analysis and the development of algorithmic trading strategies.

NinjaTrader - Offers advanced charting, backtesting, and trade simulation tools.

FAQs in Automated Forex Trading

Common questions about automated Forex trading answered to help traders understand and navigate the complexities of this field:

1. **What is the best way to start with automated Forex trading?**

    - Start by learning the basics of Forex trading, choose a reputable trading platform, and begin with a demo account to practice without financial risk.

2. **How do I choose the right trading software?**

    - Assess software based on its compatibility with your trading strategy, ease of use, technical support, and cost.

3. **What are the risks of automated Forex trading?**

    - Risks include potential technical failures, over-reliance on automation, and lack of adaptability to changing market conditions.

4. **Can I use automated trading on a small budget?**

- Yes, many platforms and tools are accessible with minimal investment, but be aware of the risks involved with trading on leverage.

5. **How often should I monitor my automated trading system?**

- Regular monitoring is recommended to ensure the system performs as expected and to make adjustments in response to market changes or technological issues.

www.ingramcontent.com/pod-product-compliance
Lightning Source LLC
LaVergne TN
LVHW051706050326
832903LV00032B/4029